Potentials

Investing opportunities for

everyone,

no matter the size of your wallet.

War for nuclear facilities
or
war for oil ?

E.E.J. Convens

Gaelic Victors

Copyright © 2018 E.E.J. Convens

All rights reserved.

ISBN-13: 978-1729667828

ISBN-10: 1729667821

D/2018/14.286/5

Nur Code : Pockets non-fiction
Nur Code 2 : non-fiction informative/general

No part of this publication may be reproduced, stored in a retrieval system, or transmitted, in any form or by any means, without the prior permission in writing of the publisher, nor be otherwise circulated in any form of binding or cover other than that in which it is published and without a similar condition including this condition being imposed on the subsequent purchaser.

The author and publisher reservesthe right not to be responsible for the topicality, correctness, completeness or quality of the information provided. Liability claims regarding damage caused by the use of any information provided, including any kind of information which is incomplete or incorrect, will therefore be rejected.

Always do your own due dilligence before investing and make sure your investment suits your investor profile.

www.gaelicvictors.com

Table of contents

Introduction
                                              page: 4
Disclaimer
                                              page: 6
Acknowledgments
                                              page: 7
Where to find interesting investment opportunities ?
                                              page: 8
Political Events
                                              page: 11
Kratos Defense & Security Solutions Inc,
                                              page: 14
Shoal Point Energy Ltd
                                              page: 18
Union Jack Oil PLC
                                              page: 21
Far from death
                                              page: 22
Saudi Arabia and Iraq
                                              page: 26
Notes
                                              page: 28

Potentials: investing opportunities for everyone, no matter the size of your wallet.

Introduction

In a time of economical uncertainties, it becomes more and more difficult not to see the wood for the trees. Stocks rise, stocks plunge and they do it all with such great peaks that investors are getting panic attacks. The most difficult part in finding good stocks in bad times is to remain calm and to stay focused on the goals that you had planned when you began with investing in the stock market.

If you look at the news, read magazines, watch youtube movies about the market or whatever way you try to inform yourself, it is hard to keep your head cool. Most of the time, these sources of information only focus on bad news and furthermore present it in such a way that you automatically become afraid of even coming near the stockmarket these days.

Although, there is a saying from legendary Dutch soccer player Johan Cruijff, who stated, every disadvantage has its advantage. This is true in every aspect of life, and therefore also certainly applicable in stockmarket investing.

As the market is allways right, you can study and calculate as much as you want on annual rapports or other financial and technical information of a company. It can be very frustrating to notice that the market reacts strange and very often is sent in a direction due to emotions and hypes, more than what is healthy for your portfolio and wallet. If you cannot keep your head cool, you will start to doubt yourself and will try to save all what can be saved right away. This is known as the escape behavior for self-preservation; a natural reaction of the mind (instinct). It will allways be hard to control yourself and keep focusing on the plan that you have drawn for yourself as to where you want to be or what you want to have achieved in a certain period of time.

There is no magic crystal ball which will predict the future of certain shares. Very often we can see that history is repeating itself, but it will never happen in the exact same way. That is why the results of the past don't predict the results of the future. Similar situations can show a different result due the intervening of politics and unforseen events. Results of the past are a very good indicator when you also have done your own due dilligence and have followed the political moves on the subject. Even the wheather, which can be an unforseen event, can have a huge impact on a stock when it is related to the business you have invested in.

Disclaimer

All views that are expressed in this writing are these of the author only and are not supported by the companies that are mentioned. Before investing in stocks you have to make your own due dilligence and therefore, you are responsable for your own successes and failures.

Views expressed in this writing are only informative and cannot be seen as investment advice.

Investing is a personal thing and the author can never be held responsable for investments in stocks nor the outcomes of these investments acquired by you based on the authors views.

Always do your own due dilligence before investing and make sure your investment suits your investor profile.

Acknowledgments

In my professional life I had the opportunity to see many aspects of the economy and how the economy works. After my studies in highschool, I started to work as a welder and got involved in the building of large constructions as factories, energy plants related products, special high temperature heating and melting ovens and even rollercoaster parts for theme parks in China.

As I always was interested in the raw materials used for these constructions I started to collect more information of metals and rare earths and studied them out of personal interest.

In my attemps to understand more of these natural resources, I also became more interested in related products, such as all kinds of machinery and tools. As I always try to catch a good opportunity, I automatically became involved in buying, selling and repairing machines. My network expanded and in the process I build many good contacts with buyers and sellers of companies that bought those natural resources to produce the type of metals needed to build machinery and tools. In this aspect I have contacts with all kinds of companies worldwide and have acces to certain information that is interesting when investing in stocks. Therefore I would like to thank all companies in my ever expanding network worldwide, and all past, present and future contacts.

For my friends and my wife, for their encouragement and support while putting my ideas on paper.

Where to find interesting investment opportunities ?

Every individual has his or her own interest in the stockmarket due to a particular circumstance in life. This can be related to a hobby, a profession, a political or natural event or by industrial and technical progress, solutions and innovations.

It might also be possible that your interest lies in biopharmaceuticals and related industries, which may have found its trigger with a relative or a friend that has (had) a particular health problem.

And as not everybody is interested in the potential growth possibility of a share price, it can be the stocks that pay good dividends that trigger investing in stocks. Many companies pay a better dividend then what a bank is giving in interests on your saving accounts.

In this matter, funds and reits can also be interesting to divers a portfolio.

All production of every kind of product, food, drink and energy finds its base in commodities. This book will deal with all kinds of stocks. Bankproducts as

Potentials: investing opportunities for everyone, no matter the size of your wallet.

ETF's and other derivatives will not be discussed. For many, even some of the bank clerks have very little knowledge of them and derivatives are the most dangerous of all when you don't know exactly what it is that you buy.

Please take note that the given analyses are just the headlines and this to stimulate you to do your own due dilligence on the subject.

Political events

Political events can be often a trigger in the rise or fall of company stocks.
Depending on the sector or area, this can have a huge impact in the stability of the world.
On many occasions, one political event sets another political event in progress. When we look at President Donald Trump and his speech to the UN (1), we can understand that after the mid-term elections in november, there wil come more sanctions for Iran and there is high risk on war with Iran.

The problem of this event is found in Iranian actions that took place, some years ago.
A nuclear deal was made between Iran, the United States, the United Kingdom, The European Union, Russia and China.
Since the deal was made, Iran seems to have broken the deal several times when it comes to the enrichment of Uranium. The deal is that Iran was alowed to a Low Enrichment of Uranium for the production of electricity, but they are not allowed to a High Enrichment of

Uranium. This High Enrichment of Uranium is needed for the production of nuclear weapons (2).

As Iran is not allowed to have arms of a nuclear nature, this violation of the deal can be seen as a direct threat to the US and its alies. Iran is suspected of supporting terrorism and therefore the risk that terrorist movements as ISIS can lay hands on nuclear technology is high (2).

The European Union is not amused with the fact that the US blew up the deal and wants to find a way to have European companies working in Iran without having to suffer the sanctions of the USA. That the European Union does this, shows that they want to protect Europe's weak economy. As aconsequence, they are putting the safety of European citizens at risk with higher threat of possible nuclear terrorist attacks. We can expect that the US will put sanctions on Europe for doing this. These sactions will probably give other opportunities in the future and there will be other writings about interesting investments or stocks over this political debacle.

If (as this event can chance its path due to other political intervenings) the US attacks Iran, it will be mainly to destroy the nuclear facilities which will set them back a while in the development of nuclear arms. There will be no intensions to attack Iran by ground troups, but a lot of rockets will be used for the destruction of these facilities.

The defense and security industries in the US will benefit from this war and there is a company in particular that caught my attention.

Potentials: investing opportunities for everyone, no matter the size of your wallet.

Kratos Defense & Security Solutions Inc.

Nasdaq: KTOS
Deutsche Boerse AG: WF5A
London Stock Exchance: 0JS0
Market Cap: 1.3 billion US dollar
Company founded: 1994
Employees: aprox 2900
Analysis: October 26, 2018

Financial rapport analysis (3):

- Quick Ratio: 2.49
- The Quick Ratio shows that the company has no problems to get the bills payed in the short term. With other words, they can forfill all their short term commitments.
- Also its cash and other current assets are enough for the long term payments or commitments.
- Share price was on this day 12.58 US dollar
- Intrinsic value or bookvalue is 4,75 US dollar, this means that the company is overvalued
- Price earnings is negative

- Price based on the value of the companies assets is good when compared with its peers.
- The company is reducing its debt (in a timespan of 5 years) in a high speed
- The company will start 2019 with very little to zero debts which will result in a strong rising in the companies net value
- Grow expectations of this company will be much higher than those of its peers

Other information:

When we compare following data with the companies stockprice during the Iraqi war, we can notice that since the company was founded and listed, its share price was reasonable stable since 1994 to the end of 1999 with a strong and rapidly rise from ca. 450 to 1230 US dollar in the first quarter of the year 2000.

After the war, the share price plunged to an all time low of ca 41 US dollar in March 2001. From here we see a low volatile movement to March 2003. From March 2003 to January 2004, the price per share rose again to 178 US dollar and than slowly slipping back from Januari 2004 to August 2004. Between August

2004 to December 2004 we saw a rise in share price again.

This information is important when we compare it with the following facts:
- First Gulf war (Desert Storm) and weapon inspections from 1990 to 1999.
- Further weapon inspections from 2000 to Februari 2003.
- Start of the next Iraqi war from March 2003 to December 2003.
- First year of the US – Iraqi war in 2004
- Second year of the US – Iraqi war in 2005

These data are traceable with the share prices and the rise and plunge as mentioned above.

You can check this stock easily with a google search: Kratos Defense stock.

Always do your own due dilligence before investing and make sure your investment suits your investor profile.

War for nuclear facilities or war for oil ?

In the event of a war with Iran, there is a risk that some of the OPEC (Organization of Petroleum Exporting Countries) will sell less oil or start to sell on higher prices.

It might be possible that the diesel prices soar to approximatly € 2,00 per liter (This forecast is meant for Belgian petrol stations and can be very different in other EU countries and abroad).

Some analysts believe that the oil price wil drop due the rising oil stocks in the USA.

My personal view is that this is happening to secure oil supplies in the US and to have a temporary solution against the probability of soaring prices of crude oil in the OPEC countries.

Realize that Iran is a big exporter of crude oil and that their export numbers will decrease drastically.

Oil companies that are productive in Western countries and mainly in the United States and Canada will have a strong growth potential, one of these oil companies that may do well when you go long, is a penny stock.

Potentials: investing opportunities for everyone, no matter the size of your wallet.

Shoal Point Energy Ltd

CNSX: SHP.CN
Deutsche Boerse AG: S5O1
Company founded: 1988
Employees: Exploration Company, no employees
Analyses: October 28, 2018

Financial rapport analyses (4):

- Quick Ratio: 29.45 (according the last unaudited rapport)
- The Quick Ratio shows that the company has no problems to get the bills payed in the short term. With other words, they can forfill all their short term commitments.
- Also its cash and other current assets are enough for the long term payments or commitments.
- Intrinsic value or book value is 0,25 Canadian dollar per share while the shareprice is 0,03 Canadian dollar.
- The company is undervalued with good growth potential.

- Price Earnings is negative (exploration / drilling).
- The company has no debt.

Shoal Point Energy is a exploration and development company in the Humber Arm Allochton in New Foundland Canada. They believe that in this area, the size of approximatly 220.000 acres (89.029 Hectares), an oil source as large as the one discovered earlier in Northern America, will be found. The company has a 100% interest in the exploration rights in an area of 150.000 acres (60.700 Hectares) of the Humber Arm Allochton under license EL 1070.

Another interest of 80% lays in license EL 1120, with the size of 67.298 acres (27800 Hectares) (4).

Investing in Shoal Point Energy is going long and can not be done to make a quick buck.

The company is mainly focused on exploration and when drilling starts, they will burn a lot of cash.

This is the reason why they have such a High Quick Ratio.

The deposits are the assets for companies as Shoal Point Energy. You can only speculate on the shortfall of oil stocks due to events that can cause an aquisition, or by lack of oil deposits in Northern America. With the shale oil deposits that are available at the moment, you can probably wait for a very long time.

*Always do your own due dilligence before investing
and make sure your investment suits your investor profile.*

Another company, an oil and gas company with big potential in growth, is UK based. The companies focus is on drilling, development and investing in the hydrocarbon, onshore UK.

Union Jack Oil is an exploration and production company.

According to my view on the Iran matter as I mentioned earlier, this UK based company wil probably have a strong growth in 2019.

Union Jack Oil PLC

London Stock Exchange: UJO
Company founded: 2011
Employees: 6
Analyses: November 3, 2018

Financial rapport analyses (5):

- Quick Ratio: 5,30 (according the annual rapport ending 2017)
- The Quick Ratio shows that the company has no problems to get the bills payed in the short term. With other words, they can forfill all their short term commitments.
- Also its cash and other current assets are enough for the long term payments or commitments.
- Intrinsic value or book value is 0.35 British Pound Sterling per share while the shareprice is 0.10 British Pound Sterling
- The company is undervalued with good growth potential.
- The company has no debt.

Always do your own dilligence before investing and make sure your investment suits your investor profile.

Far from death

The oil market is far from death and the oil and gas consumption is still increasing. China is expected to become the largest oil consumer by 2030 and their net imports are expected to increase to 13 million barrels a day by 2040 (6).

The extraction of the oil reserves buried in Chinese soil, has had its peak in 2003. Since then they have to rely more and more on the import of oil. Gasoline and diesel used in cars will decrease by 2040 due the electric vehicle industry that is strongly supported by the Chinese Government.

The cost effective Shale oil resources in Northern America wil make them a net exporter of oil, probably by 2020.

As the production of non-OPEC based companies can fall back by 2020, the market will become increasingly dependent on the supplies of the Middle East. For this reason, it is very important that there will be a lot of exploration and development to have a secured supply untill 2040.

The 5 largest oil consumers by 2025 are:

- United States: producers of light oil, importer of crudeoil
- China: biggest importer of light and crude oil
- Russia: producer of crude oil
- Japan: importer of light and crude oil
- India: importer of crude oil

The 10 largest oil reserves are located in:

- Saudi-Arabia
- Irak
- Abu-Dhabi
- Kuwait
- Iran
- Venezuela
- Russia
- United States of America
- Libia
- Nigeria

Furthermore, even when there wil be an exponential rise of electric vehicles in the future, the demand for oil will not drop drastically right away. As the world population is increasing rapidly, there also will be a increasing demand for plastics. As of this month, november 2018, according to Worldometers, population has increased to 7.7 billion people and it can grow rapidly to 10 billion people in 2055.

Even if vehicles drive on electricity, the vehicle interior wil still exist of plastics.

With such a population increase, the food production will soar and most farming machines do not work on electricity yet.

Also the production of clothing exists very often out of a combination between natural and synthetic fabrics. Research is going on but so far, there is no sufficiant solution yet. If the use of synthetic fabrics will decrease, the need for land to produce natural fabrics will increase. Herewith, demand for water will also rise and there is already a water shortage worldwide at this very moment. If one pair of jeans takes up to 11 000 liters (or even more) of water to produce it, then you can calculate yourself what the required amount of water will be when 10 billion people are wearing a simple jeans.

More land for the production of natural fabrics will decrease the available amount of land that is needed to produce food, which is another major problem to handle.

Population growth will proportionally go along with consumer growth. All these people will need housing and electric household supplies as coffee makers, televisions, computers and the list can go on for a while. All these products require a lot of plastics. The demand for oil in the petrochemical sector can increase by 50% in 2055. Don't forget that the population growth is calculated to 2055. After 2055 more people wil be born and this rising level will not stop in 2055 unless drastic events or strong inventive solutions intervene.

Potentials: investing opportunities for everyone, no matter the size of your wallet.

Saudi Arabia and Iraq

When the USA wants to hurt Iran's nuclear facilities, they need to have an ally in the Middle East.

Saudi Arabia is an ally but the recent problem related to the murder on the Saudi Arabian journalist Mr. Khashoggi is giving a delay in whatever sanction will be given to Iran.

After the recent problem between Turkey and the US, Turkish president Erdogan is irritating the US like a flea in a dogs furr. As a result, the USA has to be more cautious to the actions they will take.

I'm not sure if the Saudi Arabia problem can be related to what happened in Iraq, but during the second part of last month, some political shifting has taken place.

As a large oil producer, Iraq has—untill now—flared of 60% of its oil related gas production, but recently they decided to build two gas burned electrical power stations to be less dependent on electricity from Iran.

Contracts for the construction of these power stations where originally signed with the German company Siemens, but the Unite states have forced Iraq to break these contracts in favor of General Electric, who will seem to be in charge of the build from now on. At the moment, the company has some troubles with the American court. Also, stock market watchdog SEC is our concerned about the 40 billion dollar depreciation in the General Electrics accountancy. The problem for the US will not be directly the depreciation of the 40 billion dollar but rather the loss of tax revenue on this amount of money which is quite significant. Knowing this, it might be interesting to keep an eye on the evolution of General Electric.

Notes

1. President Trump speech to UN 2018
   https://www.youtube.com/watch?v=F2PiuixG0NY
2. Book: Matthew Kroenig, A time to attack: the looming Iranian nuclear threat.
3. You can find the company and their investors information on http://ir.kratosdefense.com
4. You can find the company and their investors information on http://www.shoalpointenergy.com
5. You can find the company and their investors information on http://unionjackoil.com
6. Source: International Energy Agency
   https://www.iea.org/weo2017

www.ingramcontent.com/pod-product-compliance
Lightning Source LLC
Chambersburg PA
CBHW070945220526
45469CB00007B/2522

www.ingramcontent.com/pod-product-compliance
Lightning Source LLC
Chambersburg PA
CBHW070945220526
45469CB00007B/2530